W9-BXR-457

# 10 IDEAS
## TO OVERCOME
# RACISM

Eleonora Fornasari

illustrated by
## Clarissa Corradin

Starry
Forest
Books

# CONTENTS

# THE FIRST STEPS

Hello, and welcome to this book! Together we will explore a very delicate, but extremely important, issue: how to overcome racism.

## Do you know what racism is?

You may have heard about it or experienced it through hurtful looks, words, or behavior.

**Racism** is discrimination based on race and, by extent, language, religion, etc. It can be expressed in hate speech or violence, or can be less obvious, like stereotypes or assumptions about people of color. It creates a racial hierarchy that privileges the dominant culture.

Many racists think diversity is a problem because they forget that our differences—physical, cultural, and personal—are precisely what . . .

## MAKE EACH OF US UNIQUE AND SPECIAL.

# Each one of us plays a part in perpetuating racism, and we must unite to stop it from spreading.

You've already completed the first step by picking up this book. This proves you are interested in doing something about racism and ready to learn about other cultures, which is a great start.

Sharing these ideas with friends and family members who are confused about what racism means is another important step!

In this book, you will find 10 easy and simple ideas to challenge racism. Don't worry: they are very simple actions that you will be able to apply at home or at school, as well as by yourself or with friends.

## Why not come up with more ideas together?
## You should never give up!

Now it's time . . .

TO OVERCOME RACISM!

# USE WORDS APPROPRIATELY

We must pay attention to the meaning of words, especially when it comes to the word "racism," because it expresses a way of thinking that can lead to some very dangerous behavior.

Choose your words carefully and use them appropriately in order to avoid hurting, wrongly classifying, or discriminating against people based on race.

# Words are often used superficially, which can create confusion.

While watching TV or reading the news online, you might have come across words such as "illegal immigrant," "refugee," or "migrant." These words often refer to people who have left their own country to find better living conditions somewhere else. But they have hugely different meanings!

- A **migrant** usually leaves their home voluntarily to find new opportunities elsewhere. They move to another country in full accordance with the laws of the country that hosts them.

- An **illegal immigrant** has entered a foreign country without official authorization, i.e., without the necessary permission to stay, like a visa or citizenship.

- And what about a refugee? A **refugee** is a person who flees their country for life-threatening reasons, such as war, invasion, persecution, or natural catastrophes; they ask a foreign country for help, for themselves and often for their loved ones.

# As you can see, these three terms have very precise and distinct meanings; it is vital to understand them and use them properly!

You might discover that the same word means one thing to you and something else to your friend. When this happens, think of this as a good opportunity to reflect on the words you use without realizing their connotations.

# There is a useful tool to understand if your words can hurt others.

Consider the situation from someone else's perspective, and think about how someone else might react to what you say.

This is known as **empathy**. It is the ability to identify with others, in order to understand their feelings and emotions.

Try this exercise in empathy: If you were tall, would you want to be called "giraffe"? If you wore glasses, would you want to be called "four-eyes"? If you were Asian American, would you want to be called "squinty eyes"?

Did you notice that those words got more and more hurtful as you read? Imagine being in a friend's shoes, and try to understand why they might find these terms insulting or hurtful.

If you realize that you've offended someone (even unintentionally) with your words, there is only one thing to do:

# APOLOGIZE.

Anyone can make a mistake. What's important is acknowledging and making up for these mistakes. "I'm sorry" is the best expression you can use to do this! And if words are not enough, you can always use actions.

The best way to show you're sorry is to change your actions after finding out they hurt someone's feelings. It's important to be accountable for your actions and accept the consequences. For instance, remove an inappropriate word from your vocabulary if using it upset a friend. You can also make sure other people know not to use the word too, so it can't happen again on your watch.

# 02 IMMERSE YOURSELF IN CULTURAL EVENTS

According to a famous idiom, "It takes all kinds to make a world." It's true; the world is populated by so many different people, with their own cultures and traditions. Some celebrate **Christmas**, some **Lunar New Year**, some **Thanksgiving Day**, and some the **first day of school**. Yes, that's correct; in Germany, the first day of school is a special celebration, when children receive a paper cone full of sweets, crayons, and pencils to start the school year.

A special celebration can help us discover and understand different cultures. Sometimes, these traditions are universally accepted by many cultures and countries. For example, both **Halloween** and **New Year's** are celebrated all over the world—but each culture has their own customs and events!

Learning about different holidays also helps you learn new things. .

- Does your Romanian friend wear a flower pendant tied to a red and white string? This is a traditional Romanian symbol worn to celebrate **Martisor**, the beginning of spring.

- Is your classmate Jewish? Perhaps you've heard him say that when he turns thirteen, there will be a big religious celebration for him called a **bar mitzvah**.

- Have you heard of **Carnival** in Brazil or **Mardi Gras** in New Orleans, Louisiana? Both are big celebrations with parades and costumes that are associated with the Christian holiday **Easter**.

Cultural diversity cultivates personal and collective growth!

## Why don't you ask your friends what holidays they celebrate?

In return, share what your holidays mean to you and how you celebrate with your family.

Did you know that there are holidays—such as Christmas—that are celebrated differently around the world? For example, in **Denmark**, children dress up like elves, wearing big, red pointed hats. In **Finland**, they prepare a small bundle of grain for the birds, filling it with succulent seeds! In some areas of **Canada**, children go house to house, singing in return for coins and sweets.

Also, even within the same culture, each family has their own traditions and rituals. Your best friend might celebrate Christmas differently than you.

### So why not explore them together?

The best way to get to know something better is to . . . join in!

There are so many customs and celebrations, each one paying tribute to the deep roots and development of a culture over the centuries. Traditions—whatever they may be—represent the soul of a community.

Celebrate with your friends,
discover new festivals . . .
and learn many new things!

# 03 CELEBRATE YOUR ORIGINS

**Do you know where your family originated from?** *Of course, you'll reply. I know where I was born and where my parents and my grandparents were born.*

Good! What about your great-grandparents? You might be surprised to discover that, for instance, your grandmother's father was born in Italy but spent his whole life in Germany. Or that your uncle grew up in Tunisia and can speak Arabic!

**Why should you know about your roots?** It can help you better understand your family and other people. Plus, who knows how much fascinating information you might find out? Perhaps your family's history is similar to that of your teammate, who wasn't born in the same country as you. Perhaps among your relatives there's someone who made a long journey to another country or to where you live now!

## Where should you start?

Grab a piece of paper, a pen, and a cell phone or tablet to record some interviews.

**The first step is to ask questions.** Interview your closest relatives, like your parents or your grandparents. Don't forget an older relative who may have a good memory! Ask where and when they were born, then where and when their parents were born . . . and so on. You might discover your family's history up to your great-great-grandparents! The further back you go, the more you will discover.

There might be old diaries or photo albums that can help your research too.

Next, it's time to . . .

MAKE A FAMILY TREE!

## This is what you need:

Paper or a large piece of cardboard, scissors, glue, a few markers, photos or drawings of your relatives, and your notes!

**If you have pictures, take a moment to observe them.** You could discover that your great-grandmother's nose was similar to yours or that your uncle's chin resembles your brother's!

Ask a parent or guardian to help you, or ask your cousins, siblings, or grandparents. Together, you will learn the history of your family.

# OK, but how is a family tree made?

- Draw a tree with as many branches—big and small—as the number of family members you want to include. If you have access to both sides of your family, you'll need two pairs of branches!
- Write your family members' names and birth dates (if you have them) on the branches, then glue their pictures next to their names.
    - Start with your more distant relatives: write them on the highest part of the tree. Then on the branches below, put their children, then their children, and so on.

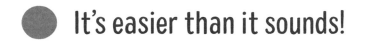

## It's easier than it sounds!

- Continue this process through your grandparents, your parents, and your aunts and uncles.
- Finally, the lowest branches are for your siblings, your cousins, and . . . you!

Can you see where you are? You are at the base of the tree because you were born recently. And the higher you go, you will find older and older relatives. Is anybody missing? No problem: add as many branches as you need!

## Your family tree looks beautiful, doesn't it?

# 04 EXPLORE NEW AREAS IN YOUR TOWN OR CITY

If you want to know something well, there's no better way than experiencing it in person!

However, it's not always possible to travel to a faraway country to discover new cultures.

## So what's the solution?

**Start with your own city**, or a nearby town, and explore—with a parent or guardian—diverse communities, like Cuban or Hispanic neighborhoods. Sometimes, several diverse communities live in the same multicultural area.

This is one way to discover cultures that are different from yours. Maybe a friend or classmate lives in the area and can show you around.

## Together, it will be even more fun, and you will discover many new things like ...
## THE FOOD!

**Each community has their own traditions and customs, including food.**

For example, pancakes have many varieties: In the US, they're made sweet. But did you know pancakes in Korea (called "buchimgae") are savory? And that they call pancakes "crêpes" in France?

Each country has its own specialties, so why not try these foods in the neighborhoods that are best at making them? Explore, experience, and don't be afraid to try new flavors!

## Are you feeling hungry yet?

Look around: There are markets, bakeries, shops . . . Observe with curiosity while you're walking. Perhaps you will notice street signs written in an alphabet or script that you don't recognize. You might also hear people talking in a language that you don't know!

You will end up in another part of the world . . . only a few minutes from your home!

● Some big cities are famous for their cultural diversity.

New York City, for instance, has many diverse neighborhoods: **Little Italy** is a piece of Italy in the heart of the city, same as **Chinatown**, with its pagoda-shaped restaurants, bright colors, and signs written in Chinese characters.

Similarly, the **East Village** in NYC is an area of the city where many Latino people live.

If you live in New York City, you can explore lots of different parts of the world ... without even taking a plane!

When visiting a new area or city,
you can ask for recommendations from
locals. Many people enjoy traveling with a tour guide, who
can tell you more about where you are and what you are seeing.
If you are traveling through Europe, look into a tour company
that pairs tourists with a local guide who has lots of interesting
facts about the area!

## Take a first step into different cultures— without even traveling too far!

# DISCOVER THE PAST TO UNDERSTAND THE PRESENT

In the past, many people fought against exclusion and discrimination. They fought for everybody to have equal rights.

## Some examples?

Nelson Mandela, Rosa Parks, and Martin Luther King, Jr.

You might have heard their names in school, or learned about them from a movie or book. These are only some of the people who dedicated their lives to counteract racism. Their actions can even inspire you today, in everyday life.

## LET'S DISCOVER THEIR STORIES!

**If today's world is better than yesterday's, you can look to these extraordinary people and their courage.**

In South Africa, where Nelson Mandela lived, people of color were discriminated against based on their skin color. For instance, Black South Africans were not permitted to enter certain areas of cities and could not go to the same schools as white people. Also, a white person and a Black person could not get married. If they did, their children were treated poorly too.

This was called **apartheid**, which legally mandated racial separation. The government created laws in 1948 that benefited white citizens more than Black citizens. These policies made it so some people were deemed more important than others based just on the color of their skin. Do you think that's fair?

Nelson Mandela didn't either.

His motto was:

# "It always seems impossible until it's done."

And he did change things dramatically! He was sent to prison for 27 years for opposing apartheid. He was released in 1990 and worked closely with the South African president to abolish apartheid in 1994. Together, they won the Nobel Prize. When the next election came, Mandela was elected the president of South Africa!

**Rosa Parks lived in the southern United States when racial segregation was still legal.**

Black people were discriminated against at this time. For instance, white people had seating preference on public transportation. Black people had to stand up and give up their seats, so white people could sit. This means a Black person could only sit down if all the white people on the bus were already seated! Rosa Parks didn't think this was fair. Do you?

On December 1, 1955, Rosa Parks refused to give her seat up to a white person riding the bus. She was arrested and sent to jail for disobeying the law. Like Nelson Mandela, Rosa Parks also spent time behind bars for speaking out against racial segregation.

Together, Rosa Parks and Martin Luther King, Jr., who lived in Alabama as well, came up with an idea. To protest segregated seating, the two led the **Montgomery Bus Boycott** and encouraged the Black community to boycott public transportation. And many did! The boycott lasted from December 5, 1955 to December 20, 1956.

It was not until 1964 that the US government passed the **Civil Rights Act**, which abolished racial segregation in public places.

# It was a great victory toward equality.

**Although we have made huge steps forward, racism still exists in every country in many ways.** So we need to embrace the legacy of our predecessors who have shown us that it is always worth fighting for what we believe in.

Nelson Mandela, Rosa Parks, and Martin Luther King, Jr., were not the only ones. Many others have made efforts to fight racism—check out their stories! There are lots of movies, books, and TV shows that can be helpful. Ask your parents or your teachers to help with your research too.

A further step is following their examples. How?

Always speak up in support of racial equality. If you witness injustice, you need to act on it.

# 06 CHALLENGE RACIST IDEAS

You have probably encountered people—even among your family, friends, or classmates—who have expressed racist ideas. If it hasn't happened to you yet, it's good to be prepared for when it does.

It's important to remember that racism is a social system, and many racist ideas are ingrained in many people's understanding of other cultures and countries. Think of it like this: Remember when you were little and scared of starting school? It's very common to be scared of something new and different. But all you had to do was go to school and find out school isn't scary at all! Racist ideas are similar, so it's better to challenge these ideas than argue with them.

Remember that nobody is born racist. Intolerance is learned.

## SO WHAT CAN YOU DO?

# Organize a sports competition!

What does that have to do with racism? Being on a team of people with different skin colors, backgrounds, or religions is a fantastic way to learn about other people. Pay special attention to how each player's skills add to the power of your team. Sports teach us to have common goals!

That is why soccer, basketball, volleyball, or any other sports you like are great ideas. Invite your friends, make teams, and have fun!

After all, sports give everybody the opportunity to express themselves, and, if you are on a team, you need to work together to win.

**Each sport demands that players respect the rules of the game and adopt certain behaviors.** If you push your opponent or pull their shirt during a soccer game, the referee can give a penalty kick to their team or give you a yellow card or, even worse, a red card and dismiss you from the game! Similarly, you can't play most sports without two teams. So don't forget: our differences are as important as our similarities.

# Always respect members of the opposing team as much as your teammates, and never insult others!

## Now it's time to play and . . . have fun!

If you like following your favorite team with your friends, being a fan is a great way to support them. So go ahead with positive cheering to express your joy and your loyalty. There is no need to use offensive words. Insulting players' physicality, skin color, or race has nothing to do with sports, which are occasions for sharing, or competing with respect and fairness. Actions and words that express hate must be stopped right away.

**Everybody, including you,
can do something to
challenge racist ideas!**

# 07 CREATE OPPORTUNITIES TO MAKE FRIENDS

Now you know several things that you can do in the face of racism. There are similar initiatives around the world like the **International Day for the Elimination of Racial Discrimination**. It is celebrated on March 21 every year.

On this day, people celebrate the world as a home to many cultures, languages, religions, and nationalities—like a really big forest where trees of all kinds grow: beeches, firs, chestnut trees, etc. You can also organize an event where people can be together and have fun!

Organize your own version of this day by setting up a themed party with your friends.

## What to start with?
## With your friends, of course!

Ask your friends to explain the rules of a game that their family plays often.

It will be extra fun to explore these exciting games with your friends!

Here are some games from around the world: In Ethiopia, they play a version of hide-and-seek called "**kukulu**." And in Zambia, they play "**banyoka**," also known as the snakes game. The main goal is to complete an obstacle course—while "slithering" on the ground just like a snake! To play, split into two teams and sit in a line, holding the waist of the player in front of you. Then, the snake can move—player by player, and without standing up! Sometimes it's played with a "gazelle," or another player that the snakes try to reach first.

Perhaps you also know some unique games that your grandparents or your older relatives have taught you.

## It's fun to share!

## During a party, particularly a multicultural one, there will likely be food!

Discover new flavors and recipes together! You can always ask your parents to help you. One friend might bring **samosas**, an Indian appetizer made of triangular- or half-moon-shaped pieces of wheat dough, deep-fried (or oven-baked), with a spicy filling.

Another friend might surprise you with a **dulce de leche**, a delicious cream dessert made with milk and sugar, typical of Latin American countries.

There really are lots of delicacies to discover from all over the world! So why not prepare a meal together?

## Mix, knead, create . . . isn't it fun?

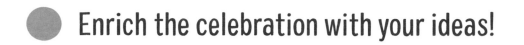

# Enrich the celebration with your ideas!

- Create a playlist of songs from around the world. Have each of your friends recommend a favorite. You might also ask a friend who dances to share a routine they love. When you hear the music all together, you'll notice it sounds a bit different . . . and a bit similar!

  Dance, sing, and play to the rhythm of the music—and enjoy all the cultures you've brought together!

- If any of your friends' parents or siblings can share, ask them about traditional hair and makeup styles. One example of this is **henna**, a temporary tattoo made from natural coloring. It is practiced in India, Pakistan, Africa, and the Middle East for celebrations like weddings, births, and religious celebrations.

- Watch TV series and films in foreign languages or those set in foreign countries that your friends recommend. There are so many choices!

# 08 LEARN OTHER LANGUAGES

## Learning another language is a great way to make new friends too!

This is especially true when you are abroad, but also when you are in your own country. You might meet friends or classmates who don't yet speak your language very well. Offer to help them learn your language and, in exchange, you can learn words in their language too!

You will discover alphabets, scripts, and sounds that are incredible and unique! There is so much to learn about communication.

ARE YOU READY?

## What do foreign languages have to do with racism?

To start, language is one of the basic identity elements of culture. Learning that "hola" means "hello" in Spanish or that "arigato" means "thank you" in Japanese will allow you to communicate and establish a relationship with someone who has just moved to your country and has problems expressing themselves in the same language as you.

### How can you start?

Play a game: choose items in the room that each of you can identify in your own language, then take turns repeating them in both languages. Whoever remembers the most words is the winner! You could do the same thing with a song.

**LEARNING WITH OTHER PEOPLE IS ALWAYS EASIER AND MORE FUN!**

# 09 RECOGNIZE AND REPORT HATE SPEECH

## Did you know that racism can happen anywhere, even online?

There is a chance you may come across hate speech. Don't downplay or disregard it, and also remember that every word used online is just as important as words said in person.

**Always speak and write carefully:** Sometimes, we forget there is a real person with feelings and emotions on the other side of the screen—that certain words can hurt. How can you stop before it's too late? Remember what you learned about empathy, and ask yourself: Are those words offensive, brutal, or harsh? Will they harm the person reading and receiving them?

If the answer is yes, avoid using them and avoid those who use them, on and offline.

## You can block contacts who thrive on hate speech.

This way you won't have to read hateful words. Most importantly, speak to an adult and ask for help.

There are designated websites that collect complaints and reports from victims and witnesses of online discrimination. Ask a teacher or parent to help. If used properly, the internet can be an incredible resource to help one another and trace important information. It is also a great tool to share words of friendship, respect, and tolerance (without offending or marginalizing others).

## RACISM AND HATE CAN BE FOUGHT IN MANY WAYS ... EVEN ONLINE!

# SPEAK UP IN SUPPORT

Maybe you've already witnessed or experienced an instance of racism. Or maybe a friend of yours has been a victim and told you about it.

## How should you behave in these situations?

It's important that you don't ignore the situation, and act quickly instead. The best thing is to alert an adult who can intervene (a teacher, neighbor, or parent).

If this happens to your friend, reassure them that they will always be able to count on you for help. This means that if they ask you, you will be able to support them when they talk about it with their parents or a teacher. And if they don't feel comfortable telling an adult, offer to do it on their behalf.

## It is important to know that silence makes you an accomplice to the act.

● **The same instructions apply if you experience a racist act!**

Talk about it as soon as possible with whoever can help you; you'll find that adults can be great allies. Or tell your friends what happened.

## The more we act together, the better we can confront racism, inequality, and hate speech.

Everyone—both victims and witnesses—can do something. What matters is acting as soon as possible.

Don't forget that together we can beat racism. All it takes is one person to make the first move—like Nelson Mandela or Rosa Parks—to challenge racist ideas. So let's work together because, united, we are stronger!

Let's make our voices heard, loud and clear!

## ELEONORA FORNASARI

Eleonora lives in a nice house surrounded by trees and squirrels . . . and full of books! From a young age, she filled notebooks and diaries with lots of stories and imaginary characters. Today she is an accomplished author and TV writer. She teaches at the Catholic University of the Sacred Heart in Milan, Italy.

## CLARISSA CORRADIN

Clarissa was born in Ivrea, Italy, in 1992. She attended the Albertina Academy of Fine Arts in Turin, where she studied painting and illustration. Now she passionately illustrates children's books, including White Star Kids' *Avery Everywhere* series.

White Star Kids® is a registered trademark property of White Star s.r.l. © 2021 White Star s.r.l. Piazzale Luigi Cadorna, 6 20123 Milan, Italy www.whitestar.it

Starry Forest® is a registered trademark of Starry Forest Books, Inc. This 2021 edition published by Starry Forest Books, Inc. P.O. Box 1797, 217 East 70th Street, New York, NY 10021

ISBN 978-1-951784-06-5

Manufactured in Romania

24681097531

03/21